Changing Life on Earth

Eve Hartman and Wendy Meshbesher

Chicago, Illinois

www.heinemannraintree.com
Visit our website to find out
more information about
Heinemann-Raintree books.

To order:

☎ Phone 888-454-2279
🖥 Visit www.heinemannraintree.com
to browse our catalog and order online.

©2009 Raintree
an imprint of Capstone Global Library, LLC
Chicago, Illinois

Edited by Adam Miller, Andrew Farrow, and
 Adrian Vigliano
Designed by Philippa Jenkins and Ken Vail
Original illustrations © Capstone Global Library
 Limited 2009
Illustrated by Maurizio De Angelis p27; Ian Escott p25;
 Stuart Jackson-Carter/The Art Agency p23;
 Gary Joynes p22, 32-33
Picture research by Ruth Blair
Originated by Raintree
Printed and bound in China by South China Printing
 Company Ltd

13 12 11 10 09
10 9 8 7 6 5 4 3 2 1

Library of Congress Cataloging-in-Publication Data
Hartman, Eve.
 Changing life on Earth / Eve Hartman and Wendy
Meshbesher.
   p. cm. -- (Sci-hi. Life science)
 Includes bibliographical references and index.
 ISBN 978-1-4109-3324-9 (hc) -- ISBN 978-1-4109-
3332-4 (pb) 1. Evolution (Biology)--Juvenile literature.
I. Meshbesher, Wendy. II. Title.
 QH367.1.H37 2008
 576.8--dc22
                                      2009003459

Acknowledgments
The author and publishers are grateful to the following
for permission to reproduce copyright material:
© iStockphoto/Dawn Nichols pp. **iii** (contents,
bottom); © iStockphoto/Rich Phalin pp. **iii** (contents,
top); © SCIENCE PHOTO LIBRARY/TOM MCHUGH p. **5**;
© FLPA/Frans Lanting p.**5**; © FLPA/Mark Moffett/
Minden Pictures p. **6**; © iStockphoto/Dawn Nichols p.
8; © iStockphoto/Marcin Pawinski p. **9**; © SCIENCE
PHOTO LIBRARY/CHRIS BUTLER p. **11** (top); © Louie
Psihoyos/CORBIS p. **11** (bottom); © iStockphoto/Eric
Isselée p. **12** (right); © iStockphoto/Maxim Kulko p. **12**
(left); © FLPA/Inga Spence p. **13**; © FLPA/Tui De Roy p.
15 (bottom); © SCIENCE PHOTO LIBRARY/DR JEREMY
BURGESS p. **15** (top); © The Gallery Collection/Corbis
p. **14**; © FLPA/Tui De Roy p. **17**; © iStockphoto/Rich
Phalin p. **19**; © iStockphoto/Karel Broz p. **18**; ©
iStockphoto/Valerie Loiseleux p. **18**; © Corbis/Reuters
p. **20**; © Corbis/Jonathan Blair p. **21**; © Corbis/Wally
McNamee p. **26**; © iStockphoto/Stephan Hoerold p.
28; © Corbis/Robert Pickett p. **30**; © Corbis/Joe
McDonald p. **31**; © Corbis/Karen Huntt p. **34**; © Corbis/
Bettmann p. **35**; © SCIENCE PHOTO LIBRARY/PASCAL
GOETGHELUCK pp. **36/37**; © Alamy/Royal
Geographical Society p. **38**; © Alamy/Marvin
Dembinsky Photo Associates p. **39**; © Shutterstock
background images and design features.

Cover photograph of a hummingbird reproduced with
permission of © Alamy/Dave Watts **main**; cover
photograph of a seahorse reproduced with permission
of © Photolibrary/age fotostock **inset**.

The publishers would like to thank literary consultant
Nancy Harris and content consultant Dr. Peter J.
Makovicky for their assistance in the preparation of
this book.

Every effort has been made to contact copyright
holders of any material reproduced in this book. Any
omissions will be rectified in subsequent printings if
notice is given to the publisher.

All the Internet addresses (URLs) given in this book
were valid at the time of going to press. However, due
to the dynamic nature of the Internet, some addresses
may have changed, or sites may have changed or
ceased to exist since publication. While the author and
Publishers regret any inconvenience this may cause
readers, no responsibility for any such changes can be
accepted by either the author or the Publishers.

Contents

Why is this flower so perfectly matched to the hummingbird's beak?

Turn to page 19 to find out!

What are some of the ways this giraffe is adapted to its environment?

Find out on page 8!

Some words are shown in bold, **like this**. These words are explained in the glossary. You will find important information and definitions underlined, **like this**.

Changing Life on Earth

Over its long history, Earth has been home to an amazing variety of species. **A species is a group of living things that can breed with one another and reproduce.** Scientists have identified nearly 2 million species alive today. Many more went extinct long ago. **Evidence shows that species have changed over time.** This book will describe those changes and the theory that explains them.

Many questions

Many extinct species, such as the largest dinosaurs, were very different from species alive today. Yet look at the illustration of *Struthiomimus*, a relatively small dinosaur that lived over 65 million years ago. In many ways, this dinosaur looked and acted very much like the ostrich, a modern animal.

Why should an ostrich resemble an ancient dinosaur? What caused some species to go extinct, while others arose and flourished? Will life on Earth change in the future as it changed in its past? These are the types of questions that scientists often ask and try to answer.

Natural facts

Scientists are not alone in wondering about Earth's living things and how they change. In both ancient and modern times, people have explained life on Earth in many ways. Science, however, demands that explanations be based on evidence, or facts from the natural world.

As you read this book, take time to walk outdoors and observe the plants and animals you see. Or if possible, visit a museum of natural history and study the fossils and other exhibits. The story of life on Earth is told not merely by words and pictures, but by the world around you as well.

Struthiomimus (right) went extinct with all other dinosaurs. Yet an animal much like it, the ostrich, lives today.

Adaptation and Variation

Each monarch butterfly has a lightweight body and thin, sturdy wings. Monarchs also store a poison in their bodies. Larger animals learn to avoid eating monarchs because of this poison. How did monarchs and their predators develop such **features**? Scientists use the ideas of **adaptation** and **variation** to answer this question.

Adaptation

Monarch butterflies have wings for flight and poison for protection. These are examples of adaptations. An adaptation is a **structure** (like a giraffe's long neck), **ability** (like the speed of a cheetah), or **behavior** (like birds' migration patterns) that helps a living thing survive. <u>All species have adaptations that help them survive in their environment.</u>

The adaptations of monarchs include strong wings for flying and a sense of direction. Predators learn that the bright colors on animals like monarchs and these poison dart frogs mean they are poisonous to eat.

Variation

While all monarchs have similar adaptations, they differ from one another in subtle ways. Some monarchs are larger or have different markings than the others. Some may be especially fast or slow, or weak or strong, or more resistant to disease.

Differences within a species are called variations. **Variations can help a species survive changes to its environment.** Should a deadly disease strike the monarchs, for example, variation within the species may help at least a few monarchs survive. The offspring of the survivors will be likely to survive the disease, too.

Both adaptations and variations are inherited. Living things pass them to offspring through **genes**. Genes carry the information to make a new creature, and are passed along from parents. Young monarchs will develop most or all of the same adaptations as their parents, and they will show similar variation.

Pet comparison

What kind of adaptations and variations are common in dogs, cats, and other pets? Try this activity to find out.

1. Find a photo of a dog, cat, or other pet animal. You may choose a photo of your pet.
2. As a class, group the photos according to species, such as cats, dogs, or goldfish.
3. For each species, compare the photos of the different pets. Identify the adaptations common to the species, and identify the variations.
4. Which adaptations and variations help make pets popular?

Homes for animals

If you want to observe giraffes in the wild, visit the grasslands of Africa. Here they lift their tall necks to nibble leaves of acacia trees. They also run quickly when lions or other predators chase them.

What would happen if a giraffe were moved to another home, such as a desert or a marshland? Most likely, the giraffe would die quickly. While a giraffe thrives on grasslands, its adaptations would suit it poorly elsewhere.

Niche

Like giraffes, every species is best adapted to a certain way of life. The **niche** of a species is its role in its environment. For animal species, a niche includes the food it eats. It also includes the food it provides for other animals.

Every species has adaptations that support its niche. A giraffe fills its niche because of its long neck and legs, spotted coat, and other adaptations. These adaptations let a giraffe eat leaves from higher branches than other animals eat from, as well as escape from predators and hide in tall grasses.

Adaptations, such as the tall neck of a giraffe, allow a species to better fill its niche.

COMPETITION

Every animal needs food, water, and a place to live. In every environment, these resources are limited. This limits animal populations, too.

Limited resources force species to compete with one another. On the African grasslands, lions may compete for prey with leopards, hyenas, and other predators. Yet these other animals tend to eat prey that the lions ignore. Hyenas often eat the lion's leftovers!

Competition serves to make niches very specific. <u>**In any environment, no two species occupy exactly the same niche.**</u> If two species always competed for exactly the same resources, then only the better-adapted species would survive.

Moles tunnel through the soil looking for worms and other food. As they do this they loosen the soil, which helps plants to grow. A mole's body is perfectly adapted to fill this niche. Its eyes and ears are covered with fur and skin, so that they don't get clogged with dirt. And its paws and claws are huge and sharp, just right for speeding through the ground!

CHANGES LONG AGO AND TODAY

In any environment, a community of living things may not appear to change from day to day, or even from year to year. <u>**However, evidence shows that living things have changed, both in the distant past and in recent times.**</u>

Changes over millions of years

Visit Como Bluffs, Wyoming, today, and you will find dry, sandy land. Yet millions of years ago, this area looked like the illustration shown at right. The climate was hot and rainy, and ferns grew tall in swampy forests. Many now-familiar dinosaurs lived here. Some ate the plants. Others were predators that ate the plant-eaters.

How do scientists know the ancient history of Como Bluffs? The clues are the **fossils** found there. <u>**A fossil is the remains or trace of an ancient living thing. Most fossils form inside rocks.**</u>

Fossils often are rare finds, but they are quite common in Como Bluffs. Conditions there were exactly right to preserve fossils for millions of years. Because of this, Como Bluffs has been one of the world's most important fossil discovery sites since the late 1800s. Remains of dinosaurs have been found here, along with those of ancient mammals, fish, turtles, and crocodilians.

Fossils show that living things have changed throughout Earth's history. You will learn much more about fossils on pages 20–23.

Dinosaurs and ferny swamps once covered much of Earth's land. They left fossils in a few places, including Como Bluffs, Wyoming. The photograph shows Como Bluffs today.

More recent changes

As recently as 200 years ago, North America was covered in forests, prairies, and other wild places. Yet, since then the land has changed markedly. Many wild places are now cities, suburbs, farms, and ranches.

Living things have changed, too. Populations of most wild plant and animal species are much smaller. Farm crops and livestock have replaced them.

Selective breeding

Where did corn and wheat come from? Why are cows, sheep, chickens, and pigs so useful? Over many years, humans bred farm crops and livestock in a process called selective **breeding. In selective breeding, plants or animals with desired traits or features are mated. The traits are emphasized in the offspring.**

All farm crops and livestock began as wild plants and animals. Over many generations, selective breeding produced plant strains and animal breeds that were hardier or that yielded more food. Wheat and corn plants look only a little like the wild grasses from which they were bred. Cows and sheep only slightly resemble their wild ancestors.

The wild wolf is the ancestor for all dogs, but dogs all look very different. The border collie was bred to herd farm animals.

Species on the move

While many wild places remain, they too have changed. One reason is that humans have introduced **alien species**, or species new to an environment. Sometimes they do so on purpose, sometimes by accident. Unfortunately, many alien species are harmful weeds and pests.

<u>**After alien species arrive, they may compete with or attack native species.**</u> Examples in the United States include kudzu, an Asian plant that has spread throughout the southeast. As an alien, kudzu has no natural predators, and has taken over huge amounts of land. Eurasian milfoil is now choking fish and other wildlife in lakes and rivers in the Midwest. Beetles from Asia are infecting elms, ashes, and other trees. Each of the aliens is causing permanent changes.

Kudzu is a vine that is native to Asia. It was planted in the United States in the late 1800s to try to prevent soil erosion. However, kudzu has become a huge problem by growing out of control. It kills native species by growing right over them. The vine grows about 30 cm (1 foot) in a day, and is even powerful enough to uproot trees if they get in its way!

Darwin and the Theory of Evolution

What causes species to change? How can the variety among species be explained? <u>In the 1800s, English scientist Charles Darwin proposed answers to these questions. Moreover, he supported his answers with hard evidence from the natural world.</u>

Darwin's ideas sparked much **controversy** and debate in his time, just as they do today. Nevertheless, they remain the foundation for the way scientists explain and understand Earth's living things.

Darwin's voyage

In 1831, Darwin joined the crew of the HMS *Beagle* for a five-year cruise around the world. He was the ship's naturalist, meaning he studied nature. Throughout the voyage, Darwin made drawings and collected samples of plants, animals, and **fossils**.

An important stop for Darwin was the Galapagos Islands of South America. Tortoises, small birds, and other familiar animals lived on these islands. Yet the island species differed from those of the mainland. Island tortoises had shells of several shapes. Birds called finches had a wide variety of beaks, much more so than on the mainland. Darwin wondered what accounted for these differences.

Charles Darwin (1809-1882) devoted much of his life to explaining the differences among tortoises, finches, and other animals he observed as a young man on the Galapagos Islands.

After the voyage

In the years after the voyage, Darwin assembled ideas and evidence to help answer his questions. He studied the work of geologist Charles Lyell. Lyell argued that Earth was very old and had changed greatly over its history. From farmers Darwin learned about techniques for **breeding** plants and animals. He also studied Thomas Malthus' ideas about population growth. Malthus' ideas said that populations tend to grow faster than they can support themselves.

In 1859, Darwin published a book entitled *On the Origin of Species*. It explained tortoise shells, finch adaptations, and many more **features** of Earth's living things.

Darwin sketched these Galapagos finches for a book he published in 1889. He theorized that each finch's beak had adapted to fit the food source available on its particular island. The picture shows another variety, the Galapagos cactus finch.

1. Geospiza magnirostris
3. Geospiza parvula.
2. Geospiza fortis.
4. Certhidea olivasea.

Evolution by natural selection

The scientists of Darwin's time recognized that species change over time. But Darwin was the first to convincingly explain how this happens.

Darwin concluded that species developed in nature much as selective breeding developed them on farms. He called this process **natural selection**. <u>Through natural selection, individuals with **traits suited to the environment survive. They reproduce, and pass those traits to their offspring.**</u> To state this idea another way, nature selects the variations among species that are most able to survive. The other species die out. Darwin called this idea **survival of the fittest**.

Darwin also argued that natural selection could change species so much that they could become new species. The theory that new species arise from old ones is called **evolution**. Both natural selection and selective breeding are methods of evolution and can lead to new species.

What Darwin's theory explains

The theory of evolution explains much about Earth's living things, including their wide variety of adaptations. The fiercest lions, the fastest antelopes, the longest-necked giraffes—each won competitions for resources over less-fit members of their species. The survivors passed their traits to the next generations.

The theory also explains why island species differ from those on the mainland. When an animal population settled an island, as tortoises and finches settled the Galapagos, they evolved separately from mainland species. This happened because of the island's isolation and because of its unique environment.

Try this:

How can the environment change a species that lives there? Model evolution with this activity.

Materials: Old magazines, poster board, small counters of green, white, blue, and brown.

1. Search the magazines and clip photographs of scenes in nature. Choose scenes that have colors that match the counters, such as a green forest, a white tundra, blue ocean, and sandy desert. Tape the scenes on poster board.
2. Place 5 counters of each color randomly on the photographs.
3. For 15 seconds, have a partner scan the poster board and remove any counters he or she sees. Record the number of counters remaining for each color.
4. For each remaining counter, add another counter of the same color to the poster. Then repeat Step 3. Do this at least five times.
5. How did the counter population change over time? What does it show about survival of the fittest?

A "saddle-back" shell shape evolved in one tortoise species. This shell shape allows the tortoise to reach food above ground level.

Radiation

As you read earlier, Darwin observed many species of Galapagos finches. Each species had a beak shape that was ideal for eating a particular type of seed or nut. As Darwin concluded, the finches all evolved from a single finch species. That species had settled the islands sometime in the past.

Darwin's finches are an example of **adaptive radiation**. <u>Adaptive radiation is a process in which a single species rapidly gives rise to several new species.</u> It often occurs in places where niches are open. Some of these places can include a newly-formed island or a newly-filled lake.

Other kinds of evolutionary radiation take place more gradually or across many places. For example, after the dinosaurs went extinct, a wide variety of mammals evolved from only a few mammal species. Another example is the evolution of **arthropods** (group of animals made up of insects and their relatives) to include insects on land and crabs and lobsters in the ocean. They **radiated** from a few species into many diverse ones.

Arthropods include both land-dwelling insects and water-dwelling lobsters and other **crustaceans**. All arthropods evolved from a single ancestor.

Co-evolution

The thin, curved beak of a hummingbird is just the right size and shape to fit inside certain flowers, such as the heliconia. The hummingbird sips a sweet liquid called nectar from these flowers. The flowers also benefit from the visit. The hummingbird spreads pollen from flower to flower, helping the plant reproduce.

Which evolved first: the curved beak of the hummingbird or the curved shape of the flower? The answer is that they evolved together. This is an example of co-evolution. <u>In co-evolution, species that affect one another evolve related traits at the same time.</u> As one species changes, the other changes to match it.

The shape of a hummingbird's beak evolved at the same time as the flowers it visits, an example of co-evolution.

Evidence for Evolution

Darwin amassed all sorts of evidence for his theory of evolution. In the years since, scientists have added even more evidence. Some of this evidence is in the form of new fossil finds, as well as new technology for studying fossils. Other evidence comes from ideas and technology that no one imagined in Darwin's time.

Paleontologists are scientists who study ancient life. They work to expand and interpret the fossil record.

Evidence from fossils

Most ancient living things left no trace of their existence. Only a few left fossils behind. Fossils are the only evidence that ancient living things ever existed.

Most fossils formed inside <u>sedimentary rock, which is rock that was pressed together from tiny pieces.</u> Sedimentary rocks form in layers, with the oldest rocks on the bottom and the youngest rocks on top. By applying this fact, scientists can compare the ages of fossils based on the rock layer in which they formed. Other methods help date the rocks more precisely.

By dating fossils, scientists have pieced together much of the history of life on Earth. The fossil record shows when species arrived, where they lived, and when they went extinct.

The dinosaur story

Fossils show that dinosaurs lived all over Earth for a period that lasted about 160 million years. Then, about 65 million years ago, all dinosaur species suddenly went extinct. No dinosaur fossils are found in rocks younger than 65 million years old.

Fossils also show that birds appeared after the dinosaurs. They evolved either from small dinosaurs or dinosaur ancestors.

This band of rock marks the time that the dinosaurs went extinct. No dinosaur fossils are found in rocks above this band.

Comparing anatomy

What can a fossil bone reveal about the animal that left it behind? **Scientists learn about ancient animals by comparing fossil bones to the bones of living animals.** This is how a skilled paleontologist can identify a fossil bone as the remains of a finger, toe, spine, or other body part of an ancient animal.

Comparing fossils from many ancient species can show a line of evolutionary history. For example, scientists have found and compared fossil leg bones from several ancestors of the horse. They show that an early horse ancestor was quite small. It evolved gradually to the larger horses of today.

Fossil leg bones show how the horse evolved gradually from smaller ancestors.

Homologous structure

Scientists also compare the bones among animal species alive today. For example, the illustration shows a certain set of bones for three different animals: the hand of a monkey, the wing of a bat, and the flipper of a dolphin.

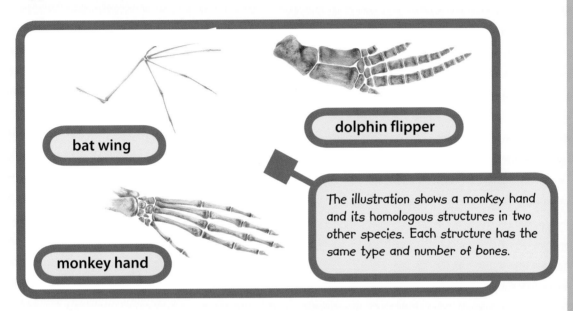

bat wing

dolphin flipper

monkey hand

The illustration shows a monkey hand and its homologous structures in two other species. Each structure has the same type and number of bones.

Each of these body parts is used for a different purpose. Yet the bones inside them are remarkably similar to one another. All have a relatively long bone at their base, then two other bones, then a set of many smaller bones.

The similarity suggests that all of these animals share the same ancestor somewhere in their evolutionary history.

The three body parts shown in the diagram are examples of **homologous structures. Homologous structures have different purposes in different species, but share the same evolutionary origin.** They may show the evolutionary relationship between species. They also help scientists infer how a species evolved.

Evidence in DNA

After Darwin's time, scientists began explaining **inheritance** in terms of units called **genes**. They also discovered the **molecule** that codes for genes. This molecule is **DNA**. Genes are the information-carriers that cause parents to pass traits (like dimples) on to their children. DNA is the structure that contains each organism's unique pattern of genes.

Scientists now have studied DNA from a huge number of species. Their work shows that DNA works almost identically in all species, and it is also very similar among certain species. For example, a difference of only 5 per cent separates human DNA from that of the chimpanzee.

When interpreted properly, DNA acts as a record of evolution, much as fossils do. By comparing DNA among species, scientists can infer evolutionary relationships. Two species with very similar DNA are inferred to be close relatives.

Mutations

The study of DNA also suggests how variations are introduced into a species. When a parent makes copies of its DNA to pass to offspring, sometimes the new DNA is copied with a slight change. This change is called a **mutation**.

According to Darwin's theory of evolution, mutations occur randomly and act to increase the variation within a species. Any variation that provides an advantage is likely to become more common in the species.

Today, scientists are questioning whether mutations always occur randomly. Results of some experiments suggest that mutations may happen more quickly when a species is under stress. This would speed up the rate of evolutionary change.

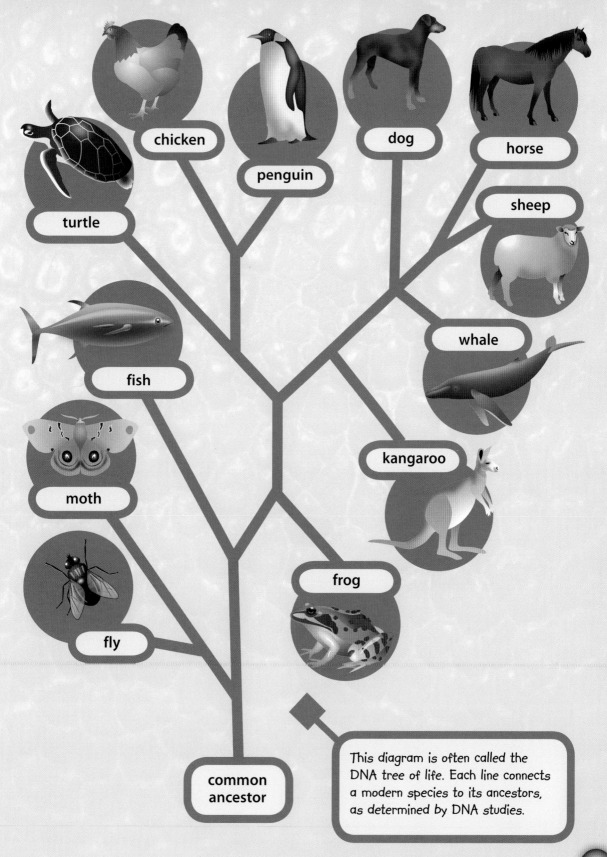

chicken

penguin

turtle

dog

horse

sheep

fish

whale

moth

kangaroo

fly

frog

common ancestor

This diagram is often called the DNA tree of life. Each line connects a modern species to its ancestors, as determined by DNA studies.

Stephen Jay Gould

If you want to learn more about **evolution**, read *Ever Since Darwin* or *The Panda's Thumb*. These books and many others were written by Stephen Jay Gould. Gould was a renowned scientist, as well as an accomplished writer, speaker, and teacher.

As a boy, Gould was fascinated by the dinosaur exhibits at a museum in New York City. Those feelings inspired him to be a paleontologist, a scientist who studies **fossils**. After years of study at Antioch College and Columbia University, he had achieved that goal.

Although Charles Darwin was one of Gould's lifelong heroes, Gould was not afraid to question Darwin's theories and to offer revisions. Today, one of Gould's revisions is an especially important contribution to the modern understanding of evolution.

I was lucky to wander into evolutionary theory, one of the most exciting and important of all scientific fields. I had never heard of it when I started... I was simply awed by dinosaurs.

Stephen Jay Gould (1941-2002)

Punctuated equilibrium

Darwin argued that evolution happened only in small steps from one generation to the next. The evolution of the size of horses, from small to large, is an example of gradual change, as shown on page 22.

Yet even in Darwin's time, the fossil record did not always support the idea of consistent, gradual change in species. Darwin argued that the fossil record was incomplete. He predicted that fossil discoveries in the future would "fill the gaps" in many lines of evolution. That prediction has proven correct in some cases, but not in others.

Gould claimed that on this point, Darwin was not correct. Gould argued that the speed of evolution could easily change over time. The idea is known as **punctuated equilibrium**. **In a pattern of punctuated equilibrium, a species stays mostly unchanged for millions of years, then evolves relatively quickly.**

Gradualism   **Punctuated equilibrium**

Gould proposed that the rate of evolution could speed up or slow down, an idea called punctuated equilibrium.

Time

History of Life on Earth

How old is Earth? In the 1950s, American scientist Clair Patterson suggested that **meteorites** could tell the answer. He proposed that meteorites were left-over rocks from when the solar system was formed. This means they are the same age as Earth.

Patterson used his ideas to estimate the age of the Earth to be 4.5 billion years. Scientists still regard this figure as the best estimate.

Earth has undergone a huge number of changes over its 4.5 billion-year history. These include changes to Earth's land, oceans, climate, and living things.

The Barringer Meteorite Crater in Arizona stretches almost 1.6 kilometers (1 mile) across and 174 meters (570 feet) deep. Large meteorites seldom strike Earth's surface. Yet when they do strike, they can cause much damage and great changes.

Geologic eras

Paleontologists divide Earth's history into four eras. They divide each era into units called periods. In order, the four eras are the Precambrian, Paleozoic, Mesozoic, and Cenozoic.

The first era, the Precambrian, was by far the longest. It covered all but the most recent half a billion years.

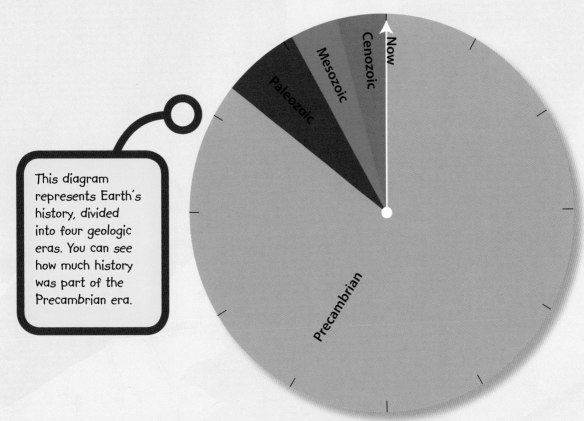

This diagram represents Earth's history, divided into four geologic eras. You can see how much history was part of the Precambrian era.

Mass extinctions

Each era and period is marked by many years of little change. Yet they also included sudden, violent events, such as meteorite strikes. Events like these are often accompanied by a **mass extinction**. <u>In a mass extinction, a large number of species go extinct at once.</u> The most recent mass extinction took place at the end of the Mesozoic, when all dinosaurs and many other species died out.

Mass extinctions often mark the end of one era or period and the beginning of another. They also open **niches** that new species evolve into.

Mammals

Mammals are the class of animals that have body hair and that make milk for their young. Humans are mammals. So are wolves, lions, horses, deer, mice, and many other species.

Early mammals, however, were not especially large or diverse. The first mammals were small and rodent-like, similar to tree shrews of today. They appeared during the Mesozoic Era, when dinosaurs dominated Earth's land.

Like the tree shrew, early mammals were small, hairy, and ate insects and other small animals.

The fate of mammals changed when a dramatic event ended the Mesozoic Era about 65 million years ago. Evidence suggests that an asteroid struck Earth in land that is now Mexico. The impact launched huge amounts of rock and dust into the atmosphere. Plants died all over Earth, and so did the dinosaurs that ate them. Soon dinosaurs and many other species went extinct. But mammals survived.

During the era that followed, Earth became cooler and drier. **Mammals thrived in the new climate and began filling niches that dinosaurs had left open.** Over time, they adapted to live in environments across the planet. The result is the wide variety of mammals observed today.

THE INCREDIBLE PLATYPUS

What animal lays eggs, has a bill like a duck, and has a tail like a beaver? It's the platypus, a very unusual mammal. Although young platypuses hatch from eggs, they feed on milk that their mother makes.

Egg-laying mammals branched away from other mammals during the Mesozoic Era. **The platypus is one of the few remaining species of the egg-laying branch of mammals.** It shows that a single animal can combine features that are typical of reptiles, birds, and mammals.

ERAS OF EARTH'S HISTORY

The four geologic eras are characterized by specific environments, climates, and types of living things. Yet Earth changed greatly during each era. The illustrations and captions show only a glimpse into the long and complex history of living things.

Precambrian

- Earth formed and cooled.
- A planet-sized rock struck Earth, forming the Moon.
- The first **bacteria** (a kind of single-cell organism) formed.
- **Algae** (a group of simple, nonflowering plants) formed, adding oxygen to the atmosphere.

Paleozoic

- Fish began filling the oceans.
- Forests of primitive plants grew on land.
- The first cone-bearing plants developed.
- The first reptiles developed.

Mesozoic

- **Mass extinctions** both began and ended this era.
- Dinosaurs dominated all lands.
- Insects and flowering plants spread across the land.
- The first mammals appeared.

Cenozoic

- Extinction of dinosaurs allowed mammals and birds to **radiate** and thrive.
- Cool climate is marked by several ice ages.
- Humans evolved from **primate** ancestors (see page 34).
- Modern humans use fuels like coal. These **fossil fuels** formed from the remains of Paleozoic life.

Human Ancestors

Scientists **classify** humans in an order (a specific level used to group living things) of mammals called the **primates**. Like many orders of mammals, the first primates evolved in the Mesozoic Era. Since then, different branches evolved into the primate species of today, including lemurs, monkeys, apes, and humans.

Scientists use the term **hominid** to describe both humans and the human-like species of the past. As you will discover, there are many hominid species. Scientists continue to research how they evolved.

Humans did not evolve from apes or chimps. Rather, all primates evolved from a common ancestor.

Australopithecines

About 3 million years ago, much of Africa was becoming cooler and drier. Jungles turned into open grasslands, called savannas. Into this environment evolved early hominids called australopithecines.

Unlike other primates of the time, australopithecines walked on two legs. Their brains, however, were about a third the size of the human brain of today. Scientists sometimes describe australopithecines as human from the waist down and ape from the waist up.

For the last million or so years of their existence, the ausralopithecines lived alongside several other types of hominids. Then they went extinct quite suddenly.

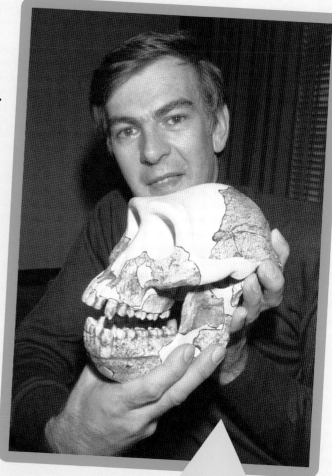

Homo habilis

About two million years ago, early homo species evolved in Africa. *Homo* is the Latin word for man.

The first homo species may have been *Homo habilis*, meaning "handy man." These hominids were able to use simple tools, such as sticks and rocks. In many ways they looked and acted like chimpanzees. Yet their brains were much larger than those of their australopithecine neighbors.

In 1974, scientists discovered fossils of an australopithecine that they named Lucy. Lucy is over 3 million years old and was discovered in Ethiopia's Awash Valley.

Homo erectus

Homo erectus evolved in Africa about 2 million years ago. It may have been the first of the hominids to leave Africa. Its **fossils** have been found in Europe and Asia.

Compared to earlier hominids, *Homo erectus* was quite advanced. **_Homo erectus_ built fires at campsites, built complex tools, and hunted animals for food and clothing.** Their bodies were much like those of modern humans. They may even have been able to talk. However, their brains were not nearly as developed as those of humans today.

According to many scientists, *Homo erectus* evolved into other species or subspecies after it left Africa. Among these species were *Homo neanderthalensis*, or the Neanderthals, which lived in Europe and the Middle East. Neanderthals probably looked similar to modern humans, but their faces and foreheads had features that were very similar to apes. The remains of Neanderthals have been discovered in parts of Asia, Europe, and Africa. They are thought to have lived from 30,000 to 200,000 years ago.

Skull shape and size is one important difference among humans and their hominid ancestors.

Adapis

Proconsul

Australopithecus africanus

Homo sapiens

Homo sapiens is the species of modern humans. They are smarter and more agile (quick and flexible) than the hominids that came before them.

Scientists continue to research exactly how *Homo sapiens* evolved. According to one theory, they arose on the plains of Africa. Then species members expanded beyond Africa just as their ancestors had done. They soon became the **dominant** or most controlling species across all of Earth.

<u>**All humans in recorded history, as well as those alive today, are *Homo sapiens.***</u> The species arguably has become Earth's most successful ever. On six continents, humans have shaped the land and its living things to suit their purposes. Humans also have explored Earth's oceans, atmosphere, and even its neighbor in space, the Moon.

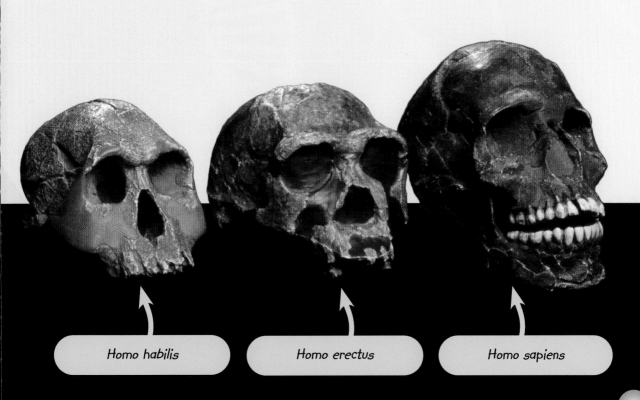

Homo habilis

Homo erectus

Homo sapiens

APPLYING THE THEORY

Why is the theory of **evolution** important? One reason is that scientists apply it to **classify** every living thing on Earth, both currently living and extinct. Species that are grouped together have similar evolutionary backgrounds. This means that their body structures and **behaviors** are similar in many ways, too.

Scientists apply the theory of evolution to make many kinds of predictions about Earth's living things. Very often these predictions have proven correct and useful.

Drugs in the rain forest

Tropical rain forests thrive in climates that are hot and rainy. Many kinds of plants grow well here, and a dense growth of plants supports animals that eat plants. This makes life in the rain forest very competitive.

Rain forest plants evolved poisons as a means of protection. Scientists are trying to identify the poisons and use them in drugs and medicines.

To survive in the rain forest, a plant species needs adaptations to protect itself both from other plants and from animals. One such adaptation is to be poisonous. When animals get sick from eating a plant, they learn not to eat more of its kind.

By applying the theory of evolution, scientists predict that many kinds of poisonous plants live in the tropical rain forests of the world. They already have found many such plants, while many more remain to be discovered. Poisons that kill **bacteria** or fungi, for example, could lead to new kinds of medicines.

If the climate continues to warm, lands now covered in cold-weather forests could be replaced by grasslands.

Changes from global warming

For at least the past 20 years, average temperatures around Earth have slowly been rising. This change is called global warming. It is causing glaciers and ice caps to melt gradually, as well as winters to become shorter and warmer in places all over the world.

As the theory of evolution predicts, a change to the world's climates will lead to changes in species, too. Indeed, climate changes in the past caused most of the major evolutionary changes to Earth's living things. If global warming continues unchecked, further major changes could readily occur.

ANTIBIOTIC RESISTANCE

In the 1930s and 1940s, doctors began using a relatively new drug called penicillin. Penicillin was the first antibiotic, meaning a drug that helped the body kill bacteria. Penicillin was very effective and saved many lives.

Yet over time, penicillin became less and less useful. The reason is that bacteria evolved resistance to it. Every time penicillin was used, a fraction of bacteria survived its effect. The survivors then reproduced, passing their traits to offspring. Today, many disease-causing bacteria are resistant to the original form of penicillin, which doctors no longer use.

Bacteria have also become resistant to other antibiotics. This change to bacteria populations is a classic example of evolution. As the bacteria's environment changed, new adaptations became common in their population.

Today, doctors keep the newest antibiotics in reserve. The less often an antibiotic is used, the slower that bacteria will develop resistance to it.

Resistance to sample antibiotic in Europe (1989–1998)

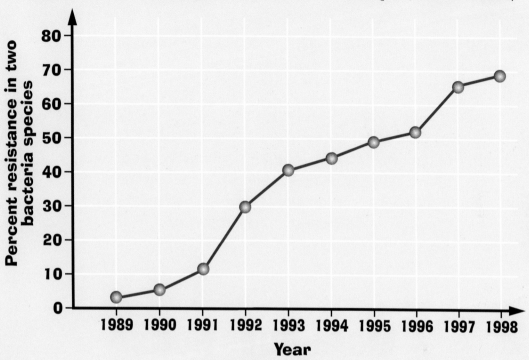

This graph shows how quickly bacteria can evolve to become resistant to drugs like antibiotics.

Summary

Earth's living things are always changing. From fossils and other evidence, we know that they have changed numerous times in the past. Living things continue to change today, and can be predicted to change in the future.

With his theory of evolution by natural selection, Charles Darwin was able to explain how and why changes to living things occur. Since Darwin's time, scientists have debated and revised some of his ideas about the way evolution works. But most scientists agree that evolution took place on Earth over its lengthy past, and continues to shape living things today.

More questions

- How did ants and bees come to live in close communities?

- How closely related are the birds of today to extinct dinosaurs?

- Why did a large and powerful brain develop in humans?

Scientists continue to research these and other questions. They also continue to review and revise their ideas about how life on Earth changed.

If you are interested in Earth's living things, you may also want to study how they arose and developed. The knowledge gained can help us predict future changes and make wise choices.

Key Questions and Answers

These questions assess five of the main ideas from this book.

1 **What is natural selection?**

Answer: Natural selection is the process by which individuals with traits suited to the environment survive, reproduce, and pass those traits to their offspring.

2 **Why are many island species, such as the tortoises of the Galapagos, different from species on the mainland?**

Answer: When species settled an island, they evolved in different ways from the species that remained on the mainland. Often the island species radiated to fill many niches.

3 **Why are fossils important evidence for the theory of evolution?**

Answer: Fossils are the only evidence of ancient organisms. They show that ancient species were different from those alive today, and they provide a record of the way species evolved.

4 **How did an asteroid strike 65 million years ago change life on Earth?**

Answer: The asteroid strike killed all the dinosaurs, allowing mammals to evolve and thrive in the era that followed.

5 **How does antibiotic resistance illustrate the theory of evolution?**

Answer: When antibiotics were introduced to bacteria populations, the bacteria evolved resistance to them, just as applying the theory of evolution could predict.

Glossary

ability skill or talent

adaptation structure, ability, or behavior that helps a living thing survive

adaptive radiation process in which a single species rapidly gives rise to several new species

algae a group of simple, nonflowering plants

alien species species that is new to an environment

arthropods animal group in which members have jointed bodies and hard outer skeletons. Includes insects, crabs, and lobsters.

bacteria class of single-celled organisms that have few internal structures

behavior a pattern of actions in an animal

breed when animals mate to produce young

classify to organize or sort into logical groups

co-evolution process in which two or more species that affect one another evolve related traits

controversy a public disagreement or argument. Controversies often last a long time.

crustacean a type of arthropod, usually water-dwelling, such as crab or lobster

DNA deoxyribonucleic acid, the molecule that codes information in genes

dominant ruling or prevailing

evolution theory that new species arise from old species

feature distinctive body part or behavior of a living thing

fossil the preserved remains of an ancient living thing. Most fossils form inside of rocks.

fossil fuel a high-energy substance made in nature from the remains of ancient life

gene unit of inheritance which carries the information to make a new creature. Parents pass genes to their offspring.

hominid member of a human-like species of the past, or a modern human

homologous structures body structures among different species that share an evolutionary origin

inheritance traits that a living thing receives from one or more parent

mass extinction an event during which a large number of species die out

meteorite remains on land of a meteoroid, a rocky object from space that enters the atmosphere

molecule group of joined atoms that act as a unit

mutation slight change in the copying of DNA that is transmitted to an offspring

natural selection the process in nature by which well-adapted individuals survive and reproduce

niche role of a species in its environment

primate order of mammals that includes apes and humans

punctuated equilibrium pattern of evolution in which change occurs at widely varying rates over time

radiate to spread out from a source

sedimentary rock rock that forms from tiny pieces pressed together

structure a part of the body

survival of the fittest idea that the best-adapted individuals are most likely to thrive

trait distinguishing quality or characteristic of an organism, such as eye color or hair color

variation difference within a species

Find Out More

Books

Meyer, Carolyn. *The True Adventures of Charles Darwin*. Orlando, FL: Houghton Mifflin Harcourt Publishing Company, 2009.

Lawson, Kristan. *Darwin and Evolution for Kids: His Life and Ideas with 21 Activities*. Chicago, IL: Chicago Review Press, 2003.

Sloan, Christopher, Louise Leakey and Meave Leakey. *The Human Story: Our Evolution from Prehistoric Ancestors to Today*. Wahington DC: National Geographic Children's Books, 2004.

Donnan, Kristin and Peter Larson. *Bones Rock! Everything You Need to Know to Be a Paleontologist*. Montpelier, VT: Invisible Cities Press, 2004.

Gould, Stephen Jay. *The Richness of Life: The Essential Stephen Jay Gould*. New York, NY: W. W. Norton and Company, 2007.

Websites

Understanding Evolution
http://evolution.berkeley.edu/
This site is a gateway to useful and accurate information about evolution, with sections for students and teachers.

Earth Science Explorer
http://www.cotf.edu/ete/modules/msese/explorer.html
Explore the rooms of this virtual museum to learn about geologic time, mass extinctions, dinosaurs, and much more.

Becoming Human
http://www.becominghuman.org/
Read the latest news on the study of human origins, or watch an excellent video documentary.

Places to visit

Science museums are excellent resources for the study of evolution and life on Earth. Visit these museums in person or online, or research a science museum in your community.

American Museum of Natural History
Central Park West at 79th Street
New York, NY 10024
http://www.amnh.org/

The Field Museum
1400 S. Lake Shore Drive
Chicago, IL 60605
http://www.fieldmuseum.org

University of California Museum of Paleontology
1101 Valley Life Sciences Building
Berkeley, CA 94720
http://www.ucmp.berkeley.edu/

Index